Heart House

RICHARD LYONS

Heart House

Copyright © 2019 by Richard Lyons
ISBN: 978-0-9964622-0-4

Cover art: Jamie Burwell Mixon
Radiating Pine, watercolor and charcoal
© *Jamie Burwell Mixon*

Graphic design: Laura Blume
www.laurablume.com

Emrys Press is an imprint of:
The Emrys Foundation
P.O. Box 8813
Greenville, SC 29604
www.emrys.org

Author inquiries and mail orders:
www.emrys.org/emrys-press

for Leah Giniusz, beyond time

Thank You

I would like to thank William Olsen, Nancy Eimers, and Joseph Millar for their endorsements of these poems. I would also like to thank all my students and colleagues at Mississippi State University, including Michael Kardos, Catherine Pierce, Becky Hagenston, and Troy DeRego.

Acknowledgements

Poems in this book, sometimes in earlier versions, first appeared in:

diode

"Autopsy with One Precaution"

The Gettysburg Review

"As Ingeborg Bachmann" as "Ingeborg Bachmann"
"Tendrils Don't Ask"
"Prayer with Kiwi Fruit and Flamingos"

Notes

"A Couple of Flies" and "The Future Is Tomorrow" both allude to a line in Jean Cocteau's *The Cocteau Diaries, Volume 1*, translated by Richard Howard.

"In a Remote Province of India," paraphrases an aphorism in E. M. Cioran's *The Trouble with Being Born*, translated by Richard Howard.

"Tendrils Don't Ask" alludes to a few phrases from William Carlos Williams' *Paterson*.

"A Natural Vision" uses a line from *The Collected Poems of Odysseus Elytis*, translated by Jeffrey Carson and Nikos Sarris.

Also By Richard Lyons

These Modern Nights, University of Missouri Press,
Columbia, Missouri

Hours of the Cardinal, University of South Carolina Press,
Columbia, South Carolina

Fleur Carnivore, 2005 Washington Prize, Word Works,
District of Columbia

Un Poco Loco, Iris Books,
Oak Ridge, Tennessee

Table of Contents

As Ingeborg Bachmann...15

As François Villon, Among Probably Others........................16

The Bell in the Campanile..17

A Couple of Flies..18

Prayer with Kiwi Fruit and Flamingos.................................19

In a Remote Province of India,..20

Hyenas and Murderers...21

Where Is the Hippocampus?..22

Tendrils Don't Ask..23

Fairy Tale...24

Gratitude..25

Table of Contents

Autopsy with One Precaution..26

Natural History...27

A Natural Vision..28

The Future Is Tomorrow..30

Dark Has Its Own Beads of Sweat..31

Not Any Less Open..32

Posthumous..33

Music for a While...34

Heart House..35

What the Moon Wants...36

speak now of mildness, now of the mystery
of salt; speak now of mediation, of mankind, of
courage; tell me that the marble of banks
can be eaten, tell me that the moon is lovely,
that the extinct moa eats green melon,

That merriment exists, is thriving,
that moss animals and mackerel shoals exist, that
means of giving up, of descent, exist, and
physical portioning out, as in poems, of matchless
earthly goods, that pity exists

   —Inger Christensen, *alphabet* (translated by Susanna Nied)

As Ingeborg Bachmann

Someone should tell the mayor the church bells
are too loud and crude. They needn't signal
the end of time. As a girl,
you lit the candles in the chapel.
They seemed a constellation
reflecting your eyes and mouth.

Once, in your car,
you emerged from an artery's smog
and saw the flag wound around the cross.

The hummingbird is a black pencil
driving off a green one
that may be its son or daughter.
Green and black chase each other
over the roof, round and round.
How can something so small
be so vigilantly selfish?
Before your mother's heart gave out,
her cigarette was a red ash in the night garden.

It is as logical as a thousand earthly cruelties.

As François Villon, Among Probably Others

I can see the fear-mouths moving, greenish vapor
materializing. Charges are levied against an alias
I didn't agree to. My street name is zero,

no capital letters—no one knows it, sssshhhhhh.
These charges run through me. I retrace my steps
in the foyer of the courthouse where fines are paid

and clerks participate in the essential act of order.
Leases and codicils. Sounds like the names
of two venereal diseases too vile to advertise.

That's why I walk with frog, alligator, and heron,
where earth and water intermingle and walking is
treacherous because the sun is timing me,

the proto-tadpole, greenish tail. Bird claws descend
while I'm out walking. Heron. Heaven. Judgments
are cruel, trapping me though I don't put a lot of stock

in what they belie or belittle. Tenderness won't let me
off the hook. Let me back among the rats and squirrels,
the pigeons and vireos, the tall grass, the dry finite scat.

The Bell in the Campanile

I'm socking the punching bag till sweat is breath,
my hair drenched. That's how reckless we are,

old hare. I love you outrunning the dog and fox.
I have ardent love for lung tissue stolen from frogs.

As soon as I learned Miles Davis had posed
in a boxer's mustard trunks, all his efforts seemed right,

breath between notes proving nothing lasts, sweat
down the creases of his nose. I hear a woman dry-cough

as if air can turn to the venom of ten thousand mambas,
as if I'm the lucky fool traversing a canal in pajamas,

spitting blood. Who could have guessed Dad's appetite
was this prodigious—is the bell in the campanile the spine's

timpani shiver? Rats crawl from invisible holes, sniff every
little pebble and stone. These rats are my beloved brothers.

A Couple of Flies

I fold a couple of flies into the concrete I'm mixing.
Red bull's-eye welts on my skin. If we aren't porous,
we're perforated, shredded, and ripped. I hear a nail gun

next-door, shingles hugged snug to the frame of a roof.
Rain is insidious, roofers say, and who am I
to refute their genius? I assume grubs call themselves

conscientious insects, feelers tracking an inch's entire mile.
The gnats fly in squadrons. My God doesn't converse
with anyone else's God. I guess the same goes for my Devil.

He's hunched over a little. Cocteau claims our crime
is being individuals. Business is poison and whole
so it's required. Attention is waning at a thousand little points.

Cities annex outskirts and when assimilated, exiles blush.
Eventually trailers are outlawed and credit cards maxed out.
Poor flies, can't you even find some diva of a blossom, amaryllis

or yellow squash bud? Rain is insidious. Flies are exact. My God
talks to me with my voice the way a ventriloquist throws his voice
to pretend he isn't the one talking, so someone can say what I want.

Prayer with a Kiwi Fruit and Flamingos

Conundrum is the first percussive instrument.
Weeds itch with treble and woofer.
In back of a gas station,
a bar of Ivory has washed many hands.

The brain is a dim forest.
Maybe a spine bends rib tines slowly.
Isn't a cracked lip a chance
to taste our own blood?

Doesn't the sweetness betray us?
The fish eagle stampedes flamingos.
The black star inside a kiwi
doesn't shine unless you cut it.

A contrabass creases my shoulder
in another life. In another life,
the sea rots. I grow so far away.
I'm Zapata. I'm Frederick Douglass.

I'm Vasco da Gama. When I discover
Lucy is a set of nicked old bones
arranged on museum velour, I recede.
We assume the blowfly mates

to praise its brief lifespan. Geese fly low,
a few muted honks. Gunpowder wafts back
from firecrackers raining on my childhood.
Hold me. Was I meant for dispersal from the start?

In a Remote Province of India,

dreams were used to cure diseases. Am I
as religious as an avocado, the meat of it
with a lightweight stone inside? Am I

as religious as a chorus declaring the twilight's
moist infestation of tree frogs? Am I
as religious as a mosquito siphoning blood

from my arm in mid-day's inadvertent yawn?
The warren is a maze of hares. The light inside
seems stained clay-yellow. Inside a dream

my dead colleague made me take the shuttle
in the opposite direction, passing beneath canes
of honeysuckle and then hollyhocks. I felt I might

never get this close again. The sun, I remember,
was bright above the proliferation of flowers
and the trundle of the shuttle made me believe in

my own birth saying the sea is a far way off,
but I must travel through the night before the light
will again lift me by the scruff of the neck.

So I let every muscle go slack and the train became
the very slackness of my body, and I was squirming
with my lips and shoulders for thick blackberries,

the bushes calling me through their individual axes
where the berries trade sight with the sharp thorns,
as if I were the forest understory abuzz with intimacy.

Hyenas and Murderers

A pack of hyenas roams a defunct amusement park
made of sluices and chutes. They hook necks.
Their whimpers are baleful, social.

I'll tie flowerets to their ears traversed by sunlight.
We can't rend the tapestry
to look only at bluebirds zeroing in on houses

with apertures measured exactly.
Sure we can, just watch us, watch us, watch us.
A few of us sleep in the desert because the winds blow

right through our wool hoods. If this is penance,
we can't say what we've done to incant it.
You tell me the sweetest blueberries are in the center

so you must reach up like an agile monkey
to fill the cup of your mouth, bushes prickly
with twilight and black flies. Lemurs squeak

in bright flowers at the crook of my arm.
I've trained one to lift the pencil and drop it
in a scarred plastic cup. It hurts to remember youth

so befuddled and distant. A cat named Samson
returns to his kill to sniff a bereft wing feather.
Once a friend shot a rabbit outside Phoenix in the desert.

The rabbit disappeared in a wisp of smoke.
I've never been so embarrassed for another human being.
I kissed this killer on the cheek. His stubble cut my lip.

Where Is the Hippocampus?

I drink a bottle of delicious artesian water. Time passes,
and we're all okay, a shiver lingering for a second or less.
I watch toadies nearby fuss with their hair in the reflection

off boutique glass. A hare's dash dips a field across no howl.
Kibble hits a dog's metal bowl. A blue fly lights on my eyelid.
I am all teeth and tail, a collision of silences and sounds,

something that can't be diminished like memory.
Is memory old perfume pressed into a dress? I defy fate
and drop through narrow cracks. Burn the ledger

and eat the ashes. Whisper precautions. Eat the beef heart.
It's a lantern you darken so refugees might cross a field.
I listen to the altar in my ear. It's a small bone the shape

of a horse's stirrup. I sniff my arm and smell my skin.
I hear a bird sing with two voice boxes. An earache
wails a cornet in its small venue. A streak of jealousy

is poking a pencil down my esophagus till apertures blink.
How long will our questions go without answers
before our voices cease rising at the ends of sentences?

How extinct is the hippocampus? The elephant? The jaguar?
If our aquifer dry-coughs, will we ask how exact God is,
will we toss silver coins to the bottom of the universe?

If manna floats like snow as it falls, wouldn't we gorge ourselves?
Must the dawn accept tears? I can't answer on the grounds I might
incriminate everyone. I prize anonymity. Erasure is the way of kings.

Tendrils Don't Ask

Tendrils don't ask permission, cucumber, squash,
or kudzu. If our eyelids are ash, will we
avert our eyes when the ash crumbles?

My eyelashes whiz like hummingbird wings.
I pluck the sun like a nickel with my fingernail.
The sunlight goes everywhere, the next eclipse.

This nest has a thread of moss and a thread of floss.
In a stiff wind, it dropped. Tact is the enemy. I expect
memory will be scentless. I can barely smell tea roses.

Will we feel the present's chill on our skin? Carlo's
mother Scotch-tapes her bangs and drinks zinfandel.
Sometimes I'm an otter, my teeth fixed on a shell

I can't open. Sometimes the world is all the smells
my childhood hay fever killed. Gardenia blooms
pierce through like perfume and the sweat of muscles

forced to burn. "English Leather is the only cologne
I've ever owned," the vague, the particular
no less vague. Want stokes a hungry ironic attentiveness

so I wait for my dead dad to come and crack my mask
with a ball-peen hammer. The mask is made from half
a coconut with broom straw for whiskers, leopard or jaguar.

My father never plucked flies' wings—a quiet carpenter.
Though he traces the widest periphery, he haunts my blood.
The future smells like sawdust. It is almost cool to the touch.

Fairy Tale

Now the barn has collapsed we can see
the moon like a broken gumball machine.

Now we can see the distant stars. Death
is inconvenient when we realize bodies

are boats hollowed out in the future's yawn.
Our ancestors are leaning in the doorways

of our mouths. Sparrows break from a field
of sunflowers, so much intimacy we're not

privy to. Lonely whispers. I don't know
why I don't die today. I talk to a dragonfly.

I talk to a rank-and-file policeman, a cop
diverting traffic around a wreck. Should we

thank the Jaws of Life? Is the blue suicide
related to the blue shark? Which one travels

lonelier distances? Second chances abound.
Ask the swordfish, a sunfish. The sun is bright.

The dead girl lies in a tub, her lips a green grape,
a bubble. Kiss her quick. Kiss the sleeping Princess.

Gratitude

I thank a boat as I would a god. I thank the fishy
odor of the cold Atlantic. A boat makes it way,
gunwales wide, my lungs stretched like sails.

In my fingers, I pinch the haddock's spine,
a clear comb. Maybe I will use this
to gather the fleas from my cat's tail. Of course,

we're all connected. My cat yowls for his piece
of fish flesh. I shot put a fingernail's portion
at the floor. As I place my palm on the warm counter,

I thank the sun at the other end of binoculars,
a yellow pea, a bumblebee, how the sun shrinks
to the circumference of a small flesh-colored pill,

whatever it takes to continue, judgments evaporated
like spray from a hose. It takes a lifetime
to love the transient, the glint of light. And now

the high-strung cat is batting its plastic ball
down the laminate as if for the Stanley Cup.
I've dreamt my infant body rushing in a cradle boat,

the reeds remaining silent, a crocodile so mud thick there isn't
even menace in the world for a moment. Can you feel that.
It's gone now, but it was a wonderful brief duration. Love that.

Autopsy with One Precaution

Close to sand dollars flecked with perforations,
close to damp sand and desiccated seaweed,
to burst jellyfish, a white one, a purple one,
close to a dead fire, a black elbow of driftwood,
the crabs weave delicacy around him.
Once, a red mullet hit his calf as he staggered in surf.
Once, he dove to touch the scales, a failing.
Now, so much is reserve, a holding back.
A necklace of wrack, brine dilating the nostrils.

His eyes like burnished lapis glance down
with false modesty and a few ounces of fear.
His teeth ache in the jet stream of saliva.
His tongue curls against the scalpel,
purple with wine. Tonsils curl
like damp stones either side the throat,
his uvula an insidious hot pepper.
Doctor, don't wipe your eyes of sleep or tears.
The lungs, two sparrows on a snowy branch,
don't sing anymore, but the blood
rich with sugar denies the Invisible
its inevitable desiccation. A note
crushed in the fist dedicates the spleen
dark with spite and wizened desire. The heels twist
like doorknobs worn smooth with travelers' hands.
The stirrup bones inside the ears shine stoically like garnets
to rock the continental shelf with defiant namelessness
one generation to the next, burning fashion, burning time itself.

Natural History

My cat's sleepy claw burst a blood vessel
in my eye, eyelashes like cilia. Much later,

in chaos-time, I'm almost hyperventilating.
Call it hack and cough, call it mustard gas,

nerve agent or dirty bomb. Give it time
and I will die before many babies, many seeds.

I apply sunscreen to the crest of my beak
or the wings of my cheeks, funerals and libations,

libations and births. Tomato vines climb six feet.
We steer clear of mambas. Some of these spit,

and we taste the venom on our lips. A rabbit
can't lift a machete or a baton, but its legendary libido

will dance with a mamba now and then. I eat the iris.
What would give anyone the impression that this

is how I prefer the world? The moon warm in my pocket,
I nibble roots. I ravage soft green leaves. Tendrils divide.

A Natural Vision

TRY TO GUIDE TECHNICAL PERFECTION
                          TO ITS NATURAL STATE.

—Odysseus Elytis

With the spring daffodils soon to rise,
your flailing around is fear of the pain
you imagine is "Count your blessings."

Maybe when Paradise looks in the mirror,
it sees something colder than it elides,
like living a childhood of snow, fingers

too numb to turn a knob or lift an object.
The lilac makes love with itself
till its spirit is a fragrant slow healing.

Red berries sweeten and the rabbits dart.
You can't put it any plainer. All thrives.
Your brain is like a house under construction.

Birds fly through it—a chill rain too.
It's the air's infrastructure a surveyor spies
through a tripod. Or does he see hands

touching lightning's phalanges? Or is it
a pirate ship slipping into a night harbor.
You're the vigilance. In the world's dream

a dentist on vacation kills a lion with a rifle.
Outrage squeezes a syringe. Mary and Jason
want a second child. A glacier sheers off shoulders

into the roil of seawater. Sea lions roar on ledges,
safe from the cruising sharks and killer whales.
The mouth's a ferocious o, the heart splitting your ribs.

The Future Is Tomorrow

I'll nurse the giraffes a team ferries across the Nile.
I will be rain the sun dries. All real debts go unpaid.
Maybe we can't transform what we are.

May I make myself energy that doesn't register?
Red ants are the brides of morning.
Will the larger machines dismantle like bicycles?

May we hide the parts among the vines, the chain,
the rims, the handlebars? Will rust marry stone?
The crime is the individual, footnote Cocteau, no,

not the submariner Cousteau, but the playwright,
filmmaker, poet and recluse. Exxon will power cars
with an algae cocktail? "The future is tomorrow."

In a short time, we will think how much has changed.
We will think daffodils clean the inner ear. They look
like ear trumpets. Watch the yellow bones of daffodils

spike the ground at the end of death's season. Death
is a hapless worm. Death is elastic snapping,
a dance we will dance. I died long ago. The goshawk sails.

Dark Has Its Own Beads of Sweat

Dark has its own beads of sweat. Dark boasts.
Dark wears its beard trimmed. I think of the shine
of a freshly stropped barber's razor,

the kind a pinkie extends as if the blade
were an artist's fine point brush to skirt the edge
of oblivion. Dark smells like cinnamon

inside a glass jar I've opened. Dark lets sounds
intrude, like thorns. Maybe it's best
if I keep my hands close. I apologize for any arrogance

I may have exuded like the venom from dart frogs.
I didn't mean anything by my clumsiness. I must say
I am unaware if I have acted in this way. I'm not sure.

O, come off it, I must remember having given offense.
Hands retract as do faces like flowers in time-lapse.
It's bright out, and I don't know what to say. I must have

presumed some right. Maybe pride is an involuntary reflex
though I doubt this assuages offense with little hullabaloo
or painless expiation. I curl up like a roly-poly when it rains

to beg forgiveness to fall all over me. Let it enthrall my head.
Whether it's dark or bright, I am in everyone's debt.
I release everyone's forgetful dream, every single, squandered wish.

Not Any Less Open

If a spotted fawn doesn't tremble the petals,
the ravenous bear may pass right past it.
My perception rips a trifecta ticket.

The unsure future is our one chance of thriving.
Jeopardy lops off the heads of rabbits.
Between thumb and index, I catch bumblebees

like bullets. I pull stingers out—thin fiber optics.
I give away loves and am not any less open,
a ferry with a leak the size of a horse's eye.

Zeal has decanted all the way out of me
into an aqueous void, a second body.
I liberate experience from words, from worlds.

I've grown used to standing apart from other lives,
memory's apple core, lime rasp, old awl.
On a suspension bridge, I devour an anisette cupcake.

I'm carrying a joey in my pouch. My demon and I
pop cold cream puffs into our mouths. Anoles
scatter across hardpan. I nose fumes. I pinch bread.

Birth water carries me. I'm on my hands and knees,
a still hare deceiving what shadows want to feast on.
Dispersal is finite. I can feel the warmth from where I am.

Posthumous

I am a lump in the bitter soup of my own body.
I remove my femur bone and twirl it like a baton.

My ashes fill a salmon's bladder
on its way to spawn and die.

I'm out to read the salt atlas without my eyeglasses.
I am necessity's hand. Who cares if militia men

hack it off and toss it into the river
like a bleeding sunset. We'll never cleanse ourselves.

Our blood is alive in every aperture.
The sun is a small welterweight—mouth guard spit out.

I can't say any of the light is stray light.
Love from the heavens.

That doesn't mean everyone gets some.
The magma is so hot the globe breaks open like an egg.

I'm jettisoning connections as I go—yeast, tapioca, gray fish roe.
Someone will clear the air, a matter of inattention mastering itself.

Music for a While

A predator spat out the horned shark—so predation
continues. Try sticking a toothpick in your gums.
I covered firewood with a tarp against the rain.

Aren't you a little afraid of snakes? Mike asks,
and I go teeth-on-teeth. Certain things startle us,
and others keep us entranced, like sunlight

warming a shoulder blade. It's music for a while.
It warns us with crescendo. So we hesitate
and then shift our positions in relation to each angle

the sun keeps. It's involuntary musculature, I think.
I'm not thinking of the moment's shrug. Sensations
arrive intermittently. And my attendant inattention is off

cherishing itself like a coral reef accreting hostile species.
Or like a goldbricking longevity waiting up ahead of us
on a switchback or on a dusty plain in Kansas. Did I

speak with the pilot wearing goggles as he fell from the sky?
Will the panther chameleon efface itself into everything
around it? Am I a gangly tourist so deep in the wilderness

I'm unaware how outside my element I am? Do I grow stars
on the palm of my hand? And what good are these unless I
give them to you, dear stranger, so you may let me go with love?

Heart House

I feed the butterflies an eyedropper's sweet.
Longevity is a dim immortal hope.

I've walked backwards for years, a small mammal.
Milky membranes inflate. What am I hearing?

Moth wings and pinto beans? I hear my heart echo,
but I can't answer it. Fear is what I can't name

so all margins imperil. We are ghosts who echo
those before us. We break a pomegranate

for the juicy sluice. We want to imagine we exist
in these fragile limbs that billow like empty sleeves.

For me to claim I know how to arrange the world
is to heave a grappling hook

and feel its weight not catching a faint lie's lip,
its world sail falling diaphanously across lightning?

What the Moon Wants

A moist white cheese fresh from the dairy,
a fresh stippling of snow, an evening
devoid of wishing, the grapefruit scent
of a Sauvignon Blanc, the voice of Edith Piaf—
who could forget her? A bright flower
fixed at the hairline, Billie Holiday—
who could forget her?
What does the water want?
It wants to lie still. Still as breath.
It wants to rush the lower depths.
The moon wants desire freed from time.
It wants the curve of a tangerine,
a guitar, the curve of elbow or thigh—
where light and dark vie for sweet concentration.